ED's THUMBSTRUM GUITAR FINGER STYLE

Special Lessons for the SOKKIE BEAT

Ed Rychkun

ISBN: 978-1-927066-15-7

CONTENTS

1	THE SOKKIE BEAT	3
2	BASIC CHORDS & THUMB STRUMMING	6
3	CHORD STRUMMING A SIMPLE SONG	12
4	BASS PICKING & STRUMMING	16
5	VARIABLE BASS PICKING & STRUMMING	20
6	BASS RUNNING & STRUMMING	23
7	BASS PICKING THE MELODY	28
8	PICKING MELODY & STRUMMING	36
9	ADDING SOME NEW CHORDS	42
	HANDY STUFF	47

LESSON 1
THE SOKKIE BEAT

Sokkie which is pronounced like **Sock ee** is a style of music and dance unique to South Africa and popular mostly with Afrikaners. The Sokkie dance is a style of social ballroom dance with a partner. It's a very cool style to learn because it has two simple rhythms that are played at variable speeds.

It is also referred to in Afrikaans as "langarm", "sakkie-sakkie", "kotteljons" and "Water-pomp". Similarly to American 'Sock Hop', sokkie, meaning 'sock' in Afrikaans, refers to the way young people dance sokkie in their socks and often barefoot. Sokkie dancers in nightclubs mostly wear shoes and dress smart casual. Loopdans, two-step, swing, boogie, social foxtrot or quickstep steps, are often danced together in sokkie. A boerewals, which is a viennese waltz is also danced as sokkie. Sokkie is not only danced to sokkie music, but can be danced to many music genres, for example hip-hop, trance, country and pop.

The beat or rhythm substitutes for the usual 4/4 (1 2 3 4) time for things like quick steps and the 3/4 (1 2 3) time for waltzes. In the case of Sokkie it is a simple 1 2, 1 2 and in the waltz it is 1 2 3. That's it because you just adjust the speed to your liking.

The great thing about this form of music is that the beat can be adapted to just about any style to give it more life through the two-step beat of country, folk, pop, and even polkas, or the one-two-three step of the waltzes. The speed can be slow, medium or fast once you get the hang of playing it. The Guitar is suited well to it and starting with three simple chords as a key, one can rapidly develop the beat to create the music and develop changing from one chord to the next in a key using a simple "run" technique which can then be extended to pick out the melody on bass (top three strings) or treble (bottom three strings) and keep the beat. Normally, in singing or accompanying others, one would use a specific key that consists of 7 chords, including 3 major chords, and strum in one chord until a different tone is needed. In this set of lessons, we are going to do the same thing adding the ability to play like a bass rhythm guitar, then add picking out the tune while still strumming the beat.

In this set of lessons, we are going to concentrate on a fast method of learning to play guitar without knowing much about music. It is a thumb strum and pick method that I use alternating between the top bass string for the bass rhythm and the rest of the strings as the treble sound. This is particularly suitable for Sokkie because you always hear the bass drum beating 1 2, 1 2 in the background. Of course there are many styles of picking and strumming a guitar but this is very simple and adaptive to any song. The key is that it gets results fast so that encourages you to learn more and practice more.

We are going to start with three simple **major** chords that make up a key. There are several chords that make up a key but for simplicity, we are going to learn with three chords.

We are also going to ignore music notes and sheet music but you will have to know the tune because that is the substitute. In the lessons, we will focus on popular simple songs in the key of G.

To play the Sokkie beat, all you have to do is count 1 2 1 2 for most songs or 1 2 3 for a waltz.

As part of your graduation, you are receiving a handy Eds Singalong Song Book that has many old favorite sing along songs. Many of these are in the key of G so you can play them after you complete these lessons; assuming you know the tune.

In this book, I have compiled many songs that show the chord line above the singing line. **But don't do the next lesson until you are happy (your fingers too!) with the prior lesson.**

Have fun!

LESSON 2
BASIC CHORDS AND THUMB STRUMMING

Guitar Basics

First, let's get the basics out of the way. The guitar has 6 strings the top thick 6th being E, the next 5th being A, the next 4th is D. These are the bass stings that you will learn to pick for rhythm and to also pick out the melody of a song. Then comes the 3rd G string, the 2nd B string and the 1st E string.

From the top along the neck are the frets numbering 1, 2, 3, 4, etc. These metal bars are there to shorten the string when you press your finger down just behind it. This creates different combinations of the 6 strings to make a chord. So you will see pictures of the six strings and first frets telling you where to place your fingers. If the finger is too far behind the fret, the string will rattle, if it is close to the top of the fret, it will muffle the sound, so the optimum position is just a teeneey weeny bit before the fret.

The finger convention that you use is the normal, 1 Index, 2 is middle, 3 is ring, 4 is the pinky or little and T is the thumb. When you see a chord configuration the big dot tells you where to press the string and the number or letter tells you what finger to use.

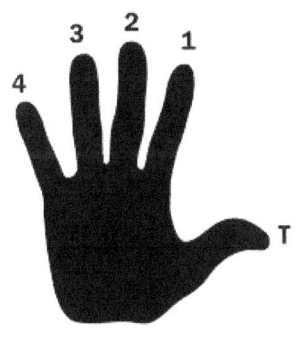

1.Your index finger- "first finger."
2.Your middle finger - "second finger."
3.Your ring finger - "third finger."
4.Your pinky finger - "fourth finger."

When it comes to how to put your fingers in the right positions, you will need to find your own comfort area but the best way is to wrap your hand around the neck so the ends of the fingers come down onto the strings in a perpendicular (or close to) direction. This keeps the fingers from interfering with each other and gives best pressure vertically, just before the fret.

One final note is to always keep your guitar tuned because it sounds horrible if it is not and when you start the next part of this lesson you will think your progress may be horrible so don't add to it. There is a section in the back for tuning.

Major Chords in the Key of G

Now you are ready to go to the guitar. This lesson is about getting comfortable with the Key of G which consists of three major chords, namely C (higher) G (mid) and D (lower). On chords, the number convention is on the big dot. These refer to Thumb, 1st ,2nd, 3rd fingers etc of left hand. The fret and the string for a chord are shown.

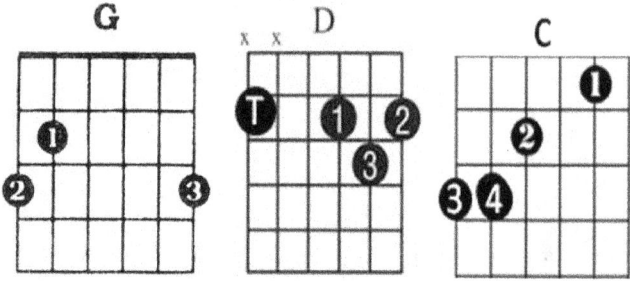

One key thing about these chords is that most chord charts do not usually give you the full configuration, typically leaving the top 6th string out so you end up playing it open and it does not sound good. So here you need to start the right way and add the top bass string to C and D chords. These give you the ability to alternate any of the bass strings in the lessons below. You need to curl your hand under the neck and try to keep the ends of your fingers perpendicular (down on) to the neck and press as close to the metal fret as possible so it is clear and doesn't rattle.

The reason to learn these chords in the Key of G is that you can use these for most songs. There are many Keys which consist of 7 chords but we are interested in the 3 major chords. For example a few Keys and their major chords are the Key of G which has D G C as its buddies, the Key of D has A D G as 3 major chord buddies and the key of C has G C F as its family.

If for some reason you want to convert some song in the Key of D, into G, you can by transposing them. I talk about this at the end of the book. But better still, just learn new keys!

Now, this may be your most difficult lesson because you will not get immediate results, your fingers will hurt, strings will rattle and it will seem like forever before it sounds and feels right. It is repetition and perseverance that wins and it is only three simple chords!

So practice a strum with the thumb simply strumming from the top string down and practice practice, practice these chord positions. First is to get a clear sound out of each string.

Changing Chords Comfortably and the Thumb Strum

Once you have the finger positions and fingers trained with a straight easy strum (count 1 2 1 2 like four strums on the same chord) with the thumb. These set the rhythm as the beats. With your left hand fingers in the G configuration, you will simply strum with your thumb all 6 strings at once to make a nice clear sound. The main purpose is to be able to change chords and maintain the rhythm of the strum. So do a G G G G C C C C D D D D G G G G strumming until four times in each chord until you are comfortable and it is a smooth rhythm. That means hold the G chord for four beats or strums, then change to the C for four strums, then to D and back to G. Then try moving to different sequences the same way, like G G G G D D D D C C C C and so on. You can count 1 2 3 4 to keep the rhythm.

This is by far the worst part and the biggest hurdle to overcome but it sets the basics for everything so sip a whiskey and persevere!

It is important to get this down to the point where you don't have to look where to put your fingers, but for now it is ok to look.

To become more adept when comfortable try do the Sokkie beat of 1 2 for each chord. Go slow at first and do G G (two strums) switch to C C for two strums, back to G G for two strums, to D D for two strums and back to G G for two strums. Try different speeds until you are comfortable and it sounds smooth… no rattles, no dead strings, no pain, just nice clear sounds. This speed changing is vital to Sokkie as it can liven up any old boring song by a faster beat.

When you can do this smoothly, try the other Sokkie beat of the waltz rhythm. It is 1 2 3 instead of 1 2 for the silent count. So strum G G G for three strums, C C C for three strums, G G G for three, D D for three and end at G G G for three.

Ok now it's time to test your strumming on a real tune.

As a special note, when you learn to do the strum and pick, it is easiest to place your right hand fingers on the guitar surface just below the strings to "ground" them so they do not move up and down. This way it is only the thumb that moves and not the whole hand. It makes it easier for the thumb to remember the position of the strings.

LESSON 3
CHORD STRUMMING A SIMPLE SONG

Now that you are comfortable with changing chords without losing a beat, let us look at a simple song. As you develop your style you can pick out the familiar songs that start in the Key of G and do the choruses. Everybody remembers choruses. For example let us take the song **Achy Breaky Heart** which can be sung/played in our familiar Key of G using two of those chords, namely G and D (C isn't used). It's a pretty simple tune but if you don't know it just go to YouTube and type in Achy Breaky Heart

When I present the song, you will see the words or the lyrics, and the chords above. If a song starts in G that is usually the Key of G in which case as you know D, G, C make up that Key. Usually a song will end in the G if it starts in G. When you see a change on the Chord line that is the precise word you need to be into that chord.

Now you can sing the song or hum the melody and apply the chords shown. Again, you change to the chord as you encounter it above the word. To get used to this do the same simple strum with the thumb over all six strings to get used to a nice even strum through the song while humming or singing. This is a simple 1-2 beat that you can try different speeds at.

The conventional way this is illustrated is that the chords are shown above the words in the song. This means that you must shift to that chord just as you are going to sing the word. If you don't know it, like I said, go to YouTube and type it in, then listen to it. You may even want to play along with it later when you know it.

Let's start with the Chorus. So get in the G chord and do a few strums to get warmed up to the rhythm you will use, then start singing or hum if you are shy. So it may sound boring as you strum but in the next lesson we will liven things up with picking and come back to this song. Do not leave this part until you can do the whole chorus smoothly and it sounds like the real song!

Achy Breaky Heart

G
But don't tell my heart, my achy breaky heart
                  D
I just don't think he'd understand

And if you tell my heart, my achy breaky heart
                   G
He might blow up and kill this man

Simple right? You are only using two chords and you only changed from G to D and then back to G. Now in this case the verses use the same chord pattern, so try a verse.

G
Well you can tell the world you never was my girl
                                    D
You can burn my clothes when I am gone

Or you can tell your friends just what a fool I've been
                                    G
And laugh and joke about me on the phone

When you have accomplished this, it is time to strum-hum a different song. Here is another simple song on called **Oh Lord Its Hard to Be Humble**. This time it is the 1-2-3 beat and it uses all three of the chords in the Key of C.

Oh Lord It's Hard to be Humble

G
Oh Lord it's hard to be humble,
G   D
When you're perfect in every way

I can't wait to look in a mirror,

As I get better looking each **G** day
G
To know me is to love me,
               C
I must be a helluva man
                   D
Oh lord it's hard to be humble.
                 G
But I'm doin' the best that I can

LESSON 4
BASS PICKING AND STRUMMING A SIMPLE SONG

The Simple Pick Strum

Now we are going to add the thumb pick part of the thumb strumming. Now, here is the rule: while you are in the chord position desired, the thumb of the right hand picks one of the bass strings for the 1 count and then the thumb strums the rest of the strings below that bass string for the 2 count. So if you picked the 6th string for the 1 count, you would strum strings 5 to 1 for the two count. There is a slight pause between the pick and the strum but it is consistent with your 1 2 1 2 1 2 etc. count.

So while holding the G chord pick the top bass string with the thumb and then strum the rest of the strings. So now instead of strum, strum for the 1 2 rhythm, you have a pick, strum for the 1 2 adding a bass note.

Now you can go through your three chords and practice this.

When you are happy with this do the same for each chord for four beats and follow the old sequence of G G G G C C C C G G G G D D D D G G G G each time pick strum, pick strum for G, pick, strum, pick, strum for C and so on.

The Simple Alternating Pick Strum

When you are happy with this you can add some class to your bass rhythm picking by doing alternate picking. If you are in the G chord, for the 1 2 1 2 beats you would pick the top 6th bass string once, then strum the rest of the strings, then pick the 5th string with the thumb, then the rest of the strings. That would make 1 2 1 2 for four pick/strum to make up the four beats. This way the bass alternates with the rest of the strings in a pick strum pick strum sequence.

Ok, you have mastered the pick strum for the G chord. Now you can do the same as in lesson 3 doing the alternating pick strum instead of the plain strum. Do about 8 beats 1 2 1 2 1 2 1 2 for G then change to C and do the same alternating pick/strum. Then go back to G for 8 beats, then to D for 8 beats and back to G for 8 beats.

If you recall you will see the importance of adding the top 6th bass string into the chords of D and C. In fact, it really doesn't matter what bass string you alternate on because when you hold the full chord configuration, they all sound good. Try it. This beat is typically called a 4/4 beat rhythm pattern like in Polkas but we are concerned with Sokkie beat (ie 1-2 1-2 1-2 1-2).

When you are happy with this try the other important Sokkie beat that is used for waltzes called a 3/4 rhythm. You know now it is the same in Sokkie except you use a 1 2 3, 1-2 3, 1 2 3 where 1 is the pick on a bass string and 2 and 3 are two strums. Pick, strum, strum, etc. As in Lesson 3, you would do this kind of alternate bass pick/strum through each of the chords of the key.

When you are ready get the left hand into the G chord and do the waltz 1 2 3 beat rhythm by picking the 6th bass string once with the thumb, then stroking the rest of the strings twice. Then follow that with the thumb picking the 5th string and strumming the rest twice. So it is a pick 6, strum, strum, pick 5, strum, strum. Now you can practice this same 1 2 3, 1 2 3 on the other chords.

So to complete this part let us do our two songs again but this time using the alternate pick strum. In this case, you will do the alternating pick strum in G until you change chords to D, etc.

Achy Breaky Heart

G
But don't tell my heart, my achy breaky heart
      D
I just don't think he'd understand

And if you tell my heart, my achy breaky heart
     G
He might blow up and kill this man

Now try this one….

Oh Lord Its Hard to be Humble

G
Oh Lord it's hard to be humble,
G   **D**
When you're perfect in every way

I can't wait to look in a mirror,
        G
As I get better looking each day
G
To know me is to love me,
      C
I must be a helluva man
      D
Oh lord it's hard to be humble.
      G
But I'm doin' the best that I can

LESSON 5
VARIABLE BASS PICKING AND STRUMMING
TWO NEW SONGS

Now you are ready to use a bit of creativity with the bass picking. You are going to use the alternating bass strum for each chord but this time you can pick any of the top four strings and then strum the rest below the one picked. You can play around with this and as you sing the songs they begin to sound like you know what you are doing!

To illustrate this we will use Kenny Rogers and two favorite songs the Gambler which is the 1 2 1 2 beat and Lucile for the 1 2 3, 1 2 3 beat. We will do the chorus of each in G. Again YouTube is great to listen to the songs if you don't know them.

The Gambler Chorus

G
You got to know how to hold 'em,
C   G
know when to fold 'em,
C   G
know when to walk away and
                D
know when to run.

  G
You never count your money
G   C   G
when you're sittin' at the table.
                            C   G
There'll be time enough for countin'
   D   G
when the dealin's done.

Now here is the 1 2 3 beat, so remember, it is the alternating bass and two strums

Lucille Chorus

G   C
You picked a fine time to leave me Lucille,

with four hungry children
                      G
and a crop in the field.
C
I've had some bad times

lived through some sad times
                                G
but this time your hurtin won't heal.
                  D   G
You picked a fine time to leave me Lucille.

These songs are in your book and the Gambler uses other chords but you can get to this later. But do not take shortcuts. Make sure you are happy with these two songs before you move on.

LESSON 6
BASS RUNNING AND STRUMMING

In this lesson we are going go a step further and do a Run between chords. We want to do the thumb/strum but this time add a Run. The run places single notes that take you from one chord to the other in a nice bass transition. Between chord changes, you are going to pick four notes with the thumb.

So if you are in the G chord, you have learned to alternate bass rhythm to pick the top 6th bass string once, strum the rest of the strings, then pick the 5th string with the thumb, then the rest of the strings to do a pick strum pick strum count of 1 2 1 2. This way the bass alternates with the rest of the strings.

Now we are going to add the Run which is used a lot in bass or background accompaniment in bands and for singing. It is a smooth four picks (notes) that take you from one chord to the other in a key. So if you were in G and wanted to Run down to C, you do this by picking four notes as shown below in red, then strum in C. So have a look at this new diagram.

Here you would start with G chord, and do a 1 2 1 2 alternating beat. Then still holding the G chord position you continue with another 1 2 1 2 as 4 beats (with thumb) using the 1st or 2nd left hand finger for the picking notes. On the fourth pick (beat) you will have shifted to the next chord of C which miraculously happens to include the fourth beat! So have a look at the picture below. In this case, the Red dots and the numbers inside indicate the <u>sequence</u> of the beats 1 2 1 2. not the finger in like in the chord configurations. The red 2 above the frets means picking the 5th string with thumb in the open position as the second beat.

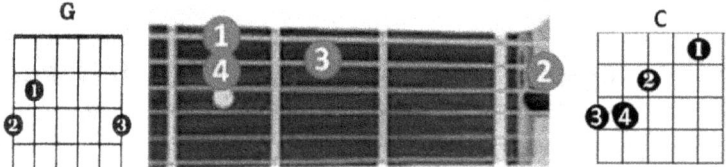

Ok let me explain this again in four simple steps:
1. You are holding the G chord and you pick strum, pick strum using the alternate pick strum.
2. The next pick is the red 1 on the 3rd fret of the 6th string. The neat thing is that your second finger is already there!
3. Now you stay in the chord position and only use the first or second finger, which ever works better and pick the 5th string open as beat 2, then on 5th string second fret for beat 3.
4. Then you must put your fingers onto the C position and guess what? It already is in the right position for beat 4.

This creates a smooth run down to the C chord.

Now before going any further, you want to practice this run until it is smooth and your fingers do it automatically. Just keep doing the 1 2 3 4 (or the Sokkie 1 2 1 2) until it is automatic.

Now you are ready to pick from the C chord position back up the run to the G position to launch the alternating pick/strum in G.

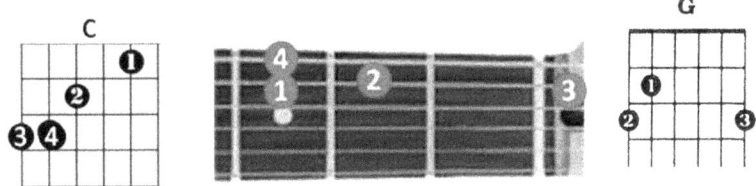

Again, practice the four pick until it is automatic. Now we want to run to the next chord in the Key of G which is D. so picking with thumb and using the 1st or second finger on the left hand you pick the four notes as shown to end up in the D chord configuration to the alternating Pick/strum in D

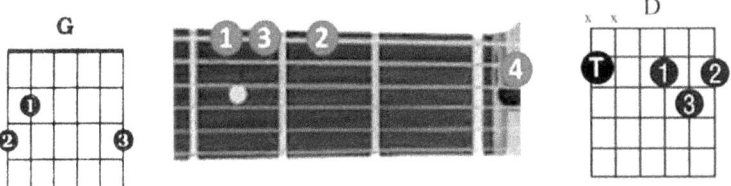

Then you runback up from the D back to the G by picking the following four note sequence.

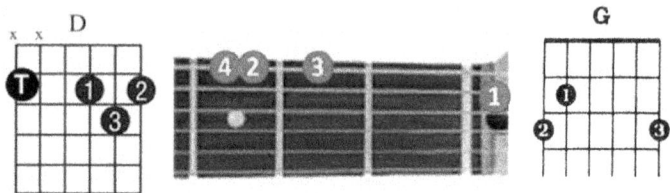

So here is the whole sequence:

In G Pick, strum pick strum
Run down to C picking 1 2 3 4 bass notes
In C pick strum, pick strum
Run up to G picking 1 2 3 4 bass notes
In G pick strum, pick strum
Run to D picking 1 2 3 4 bass notes
In D pick strum, pick strum
Run to G Picking 1 2 3 4 bass notes
In D pick strum, pick strum

Now you can try running from each chord in the Key up and down trying the two different beats like in lesson 3 with the 1-2 1-2 (pick strum pick strum) beat or 4/4 time and the 1 2 3 (Pick strum strum, pick strum, strum)

This type of Run can be done in any Key of 3 chords. Each Key is a different pitch which is chosen to match a person's voice or tone preference. So in the Key of D for example (a bit lower than Key of G) A D and G would be the chords and you would run from D down to G, back to D, up to A and down to D. This is used in doing the bass rhythm for some or musical accompaniment.

LESSON 7
BASS PICKING THE MELODY

Ok, we are ready to try something new. You have learned to pick and strum in several ways.

Now it is time to get even fancier and pick the tune out on the bass string and strum. First look at the tablature below which we will use from now on. It shows the 6 strings on your guitar and numbers that tell you what fret your 1st or 2nd finger is used to play the notes of the tune, leaving the other fingers in the position of the chord. The 0 means no fret, just pick an open string. The arrow means strum the strings but you must be in the chord shown on the line above the words. The secret is that you are actually picking the notes that are already part of your chord pattern. Now let us try our simple two chord song.

Achy Breaky Heart

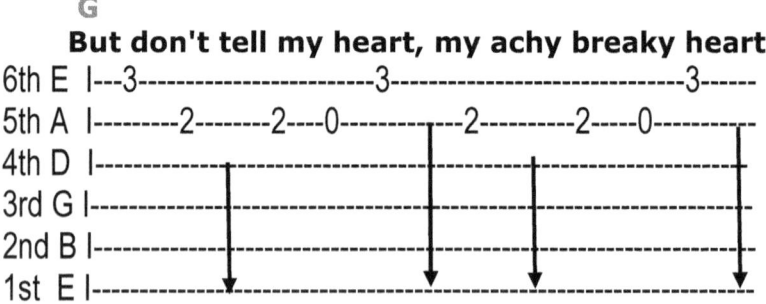

You should play this line over and over until it is automatic, then move to the next line. You will note that in singing a song or accompanying someone, you keep your left hand in the chord position until a change is shown on the top line.

It is the same here so when you use your 1st or 2nd finger to move to a note not part of the chord, you simply put it back onto the chord position.

Ok, let's continue.

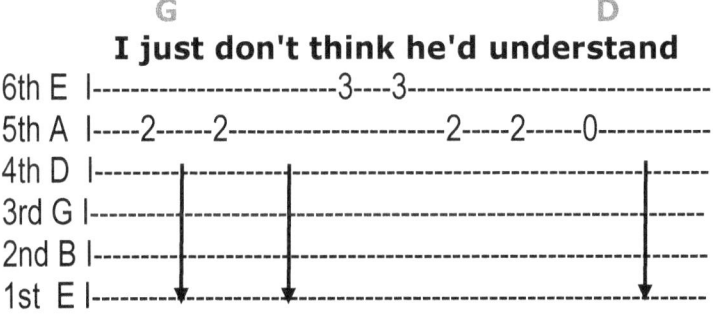

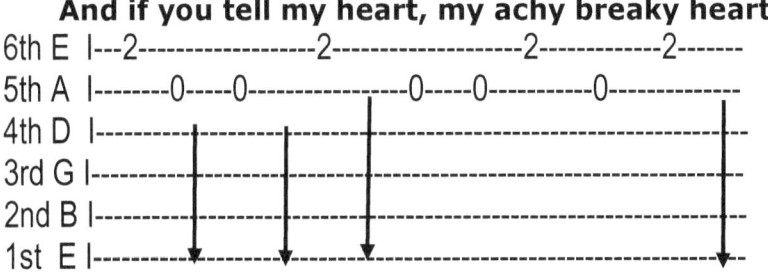

He might blow up and kill this man   **G**

```
6th E |-------------------2-----2-----------------3------------
5th A |----0----------0---------------------0-----0-------------
4th D |----------|---------|-------------------------|---------
3rd G |----------|---------|-------------------------|---------
2nd B |----------|---------|-------------------------|---------
1st E |----------▼---------▼-------------------------▼---------
```

When you have mastered this you can try the next song which is a bit more complex but it is the same idea.

The Gambler Chorus

G
You got to know how to hold 'em,

```
6th E |---3-------------------------------3--------------------
5th A |----------2------------------------------2---------------
4th D |--------------0-----------0------------------------------
3rd G |--------------------|------------------------|----------
2nd B |--------------------|------------------------|----------
1st E |--------------------▼------------------------▼----------
```

```
              C                      G
         know when to fold 'em,
6th E |----------------------------------------------------
5th A |----2----3------------------------2-----------------
4th D |-------------------2----2----0----------------------
3rd G |----------------------------------------------------
2nd B |----------------------------------------------------
1st E |----------------------------------------------------

              C                      G
         know when to walk away and
6th E |----------------------------------------------------
5th A |-----3-----------------------------2----------------
4th D |----------------2----2-------0----------------------
3rd G |----------------------------------------------------
2nd B |----------------------------------------------------
1st E |----------------------------------------------------

                             D
           know when to run.
6th E |------------------------3---------------------------
5th A |---------2----------0----------0--------------------
4th D |----------------------------------------------------
3rd G |----------------------------------------------------
2nd B |----------------------------------------------------
1st E |----------------------------------------------------
```

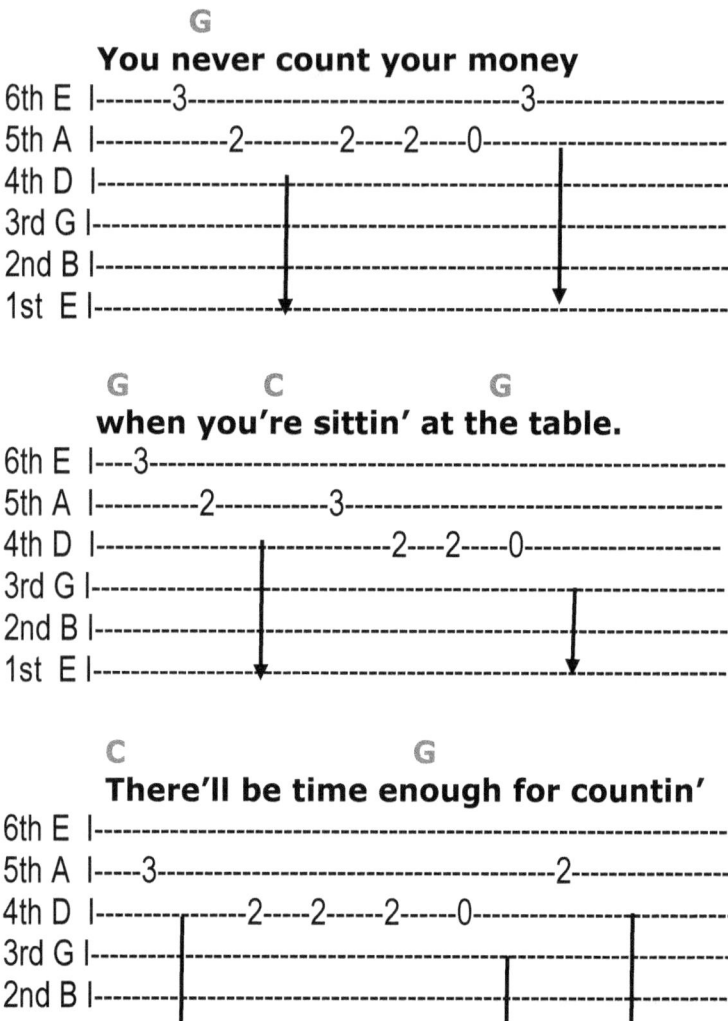

```
              D                 G
            when the dealin's done.
6th E  |-------------------2-------------3---------------------------
5th A  |--------0--------------------------------------------------
4th D  |-----------------------------------------------------------
3rd G  |-----------------------------------------------------------
2nd B  |-----------------------------------------------------------
1st E  |-----------------------------------------------------------
```

Now here is the 1 2 3 beat, so remember, it is the alternating bass and two strums

Lucille Chorus

```
     G                                    C
      You picked a fine time to leave me Lucille,
6th E  |--3----3---------------------------------------------------
5th A  |-------------2--------------------------------3------------
4th D  |--------------------0-----0----------4-----2---------------
3rd G  |-----------------------------------0-----------------------
2nd B  |-----------------------------------------------------------
1st E  |-----------------------------------------------------------
```

C
with four hungry children

```
6th E |------------------------------------------------
5th A |------------------------------------------------
4th D |-----2------------------------4-----2-----------
3rd G |------------0-----↓-----↓----------------------
2nd B |------------------------------------------------
1st E |------------------------------------------------
```

G
and a crop in the field.

```
6th E |------------------------------------------------
5th A |------------------------------------------------
4th D |----2----------4-----2----0---------------------
3rd G |------------0------------↓-----↓----------------
2nd B |------------------------------------------------
1st E |------------------------------------------------
```

C
I've had some bad times

```
6th E |------------------------------------------------
5th A |------------------------------------------------
4th D |-----2------------------------4-----2-----------
3rd G |------------0-----↓-----↓----------------------
2nd B |------------------------------------------------
1st E |------------------------------------------------
```

lived through some sad times
```
6th E |----------------------------------------------------------------
5th A |----------------------------------------------------------------
4th D |------2-----------------------4-----2--------------------------
3rd G |--------------0---------------------------------------
2nd B |----------------↓-----↓----------------------------------
1st  E |----------------------------------------------------------------
```

                                                                   G

but this time your hurtin won't heal.
```
6th E |----------------------------------------------------------------
5th A |----------------------------------------------------------------
4th D |--------2-----------------4-----2---2----0-------------
3rd G |--------------0---------------------------------------
2nd B |----------------↓-----↓---------------------↓----↓-----
1st  E |----------------------------------------------------------------
```

                     D   G

You picked a fine time to leave me Lucille.
```
6th E |-----------------------------------------------3---------------
5th A |-----------------0-----------2----3---2---0--------------------
4th D |---0----0------------------------------------------------------
3rd G |----------------------------------------------------------------
2nd B |-------------------↓--------------------------↓----↓-----------
1st  E |----------------------------------------------------------------
```

LESSON 8
PICKING MELODY AND STRUMMING

Ok, let's do one more song through our learning sequence. This is a typical 1 2 Sokkie beat which you can select your own speed on. It is best to start slow and speed up as you get familiar with the song. In this case you will begin in G and do an Alternating pick strum to your own choosing. You will find that if you hold the complete chord like you have been taught to, when you alternate your picking, you don't have to stick with the 6th and 5th strings. Picking almost any of the upper strings between strums sound ok. Try it on this next tune which follows the Run Progression of G to C, back to G, then to D and back to G. This is a favorite progression in most Country and Cowboys songs.

So go ahead and practice this one called **This Land Is My Land**

CHORUS
G   C   G
This land is your land, this land is my land,
        D   G
From California, to the New York Island,

                        C   G

From the Redwood Forest, to the Gulf Stream Waters,
  D   G
This land was made for you and me.

Think you can sing this song without seeing the chord line? The verses use the same chords so give it a try.

I roamed and rambled, and I followed my footsteps
To the sparkling sands of her diamond deserts
And all around me a voice was singing
This land was made for you and me!

As you do this, you can also practice a light strum with the thumb back up. This gives and added sound of double strumming the strings maintaining the same song rhythm.

Picking the Base Melody and Strumming

Let us now continue on **This Land is My Land** to pick out the tune on the top strings. You will see a similarity to the Run progression in a previous lesson.

This land is your land, this land is my land,

```
         G          C                    G
6th E |---3-----------------------------3--------------------
5th A |--------0---2---3-------3--------3---------3-----2-----2---
4th D |------------------------------------------------------
3rd G |------------------------------------------------------
2nd B |------------------------------------------------------
1st E |------------------------------------------------------
```

From Cal i forn ia,   to the New York Island,

```
                         D                    G
6th E |-----------------------------------------3--------------------
5th A |-----2-----3----2-----0--------0---------0---------0----2-----2---
4th D |------------------------------------------------------
3rd G |------------------------------------------------------
2nd B |------------------------------------------------------
1st E |------------------------------------------------------
```

From the Redwood Forest, to the Gulf Stream Waters,

```
         G          C                    G
6th E |---3-----------------------------3--------------------
5th A |--------0---2---3-------3---------3---------3----2-------2------
4th D |------------------------------------------------------
3rd G |------------------------------------------------------
2nd B |------------------------------------------------------
1st E |------------------------------------------------------
```

This land was made for you and me.

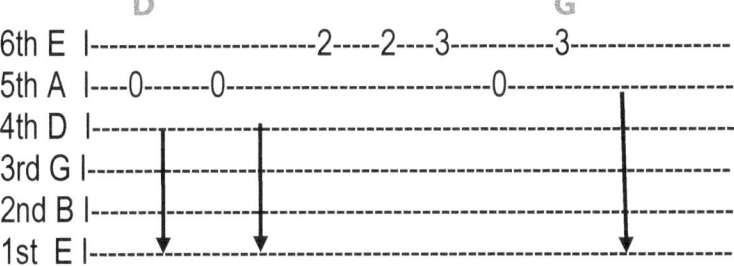

When you feel comfortable with this, you can try to use your thumb to double strum down and up to create fuller sound. You can practice with this; it is just a light strum back up all within the same beat

Picking a Treble Melody and Strumming

Now as an extension to picking the bass strings, you can also pick the lower treble strings to pick the melody and strum. Because you are now picking bottom treble strings for the melody, you should strum the lower four strings from 4 or 5 down to fill the sound.

This land is your land,　this land is my land,

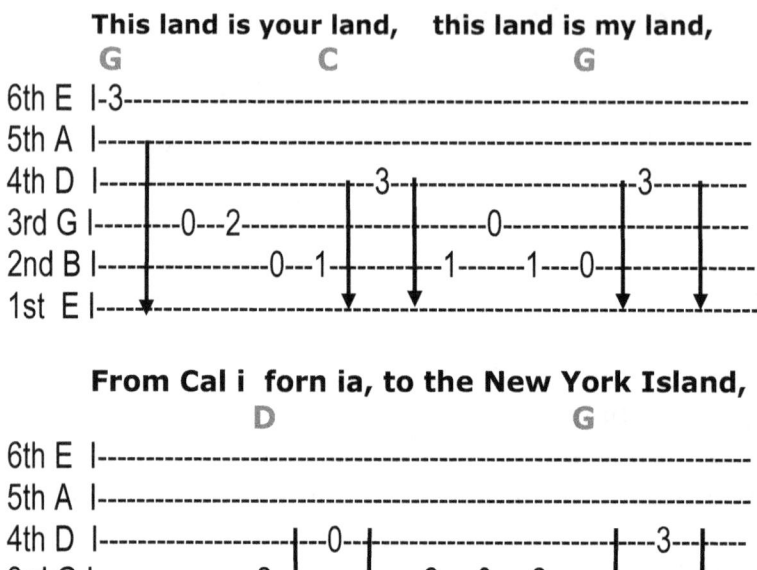

From California, to the New York Island,

From the Redwood Forest, to the Gulf Stream Waters,

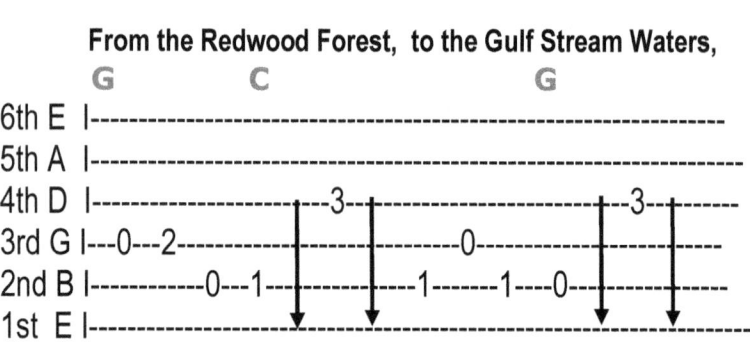

This land was made for you and me.

```
         D                              G
6th E |----------------------------------------------------------
5th A |----------------------------------------------------------
4th D |------------------------0-------2----4--------------------
3rd G |----2-----2-----2---------------------0-------------------
2nd B |----------------------------------------------------------
1st E |----------------------------------------------------------
```

LESSON 9
ADDING SOME NEW CHORDS

Most everybody knows **Don't Think Twice** by Bob Dylan so let us try it. This will bring three new chords into the picture, namely D7, Em and A7. On the A7 you use the first finger to cover multiple strings as shown. These are in support of the Key of G.

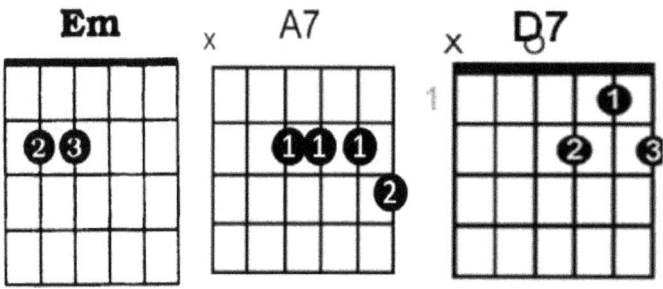

The reason I want to introduce you to these extra chords is because you have focused on the three MAJOR chords of the Key of G. This was to keep it simple because the Major Chords are good enough to play most songs.

In truth there are 7 chords in every key:
3 MAJOR CHORDS
3 minor CHORDS
1 diminished CHORD
In any key they follows the do re me fa so la te do or A B C D E F G A cycle

The music convention is that for example in the Key of G, the 7 chords are as follows:

KEY	M1	M1	M2	M2	M3	M3	D1
C	C	Dm	Em	F	G	Am	Bd
D	D	Em	Fm	G	A	Bm	C#d
E	E	F#m	G#m	A	B	C#m	D#d
F	F	Gm	Am	Bb	C	Dm	Ed
G	G	Am	Bm	C	D	Em	F#d
A	A	Bm	C#m	D	E	F#m	G#d
B	B	C#m	D#m	E	F#	G#m	A#m

Here is the full family for the Key of G.

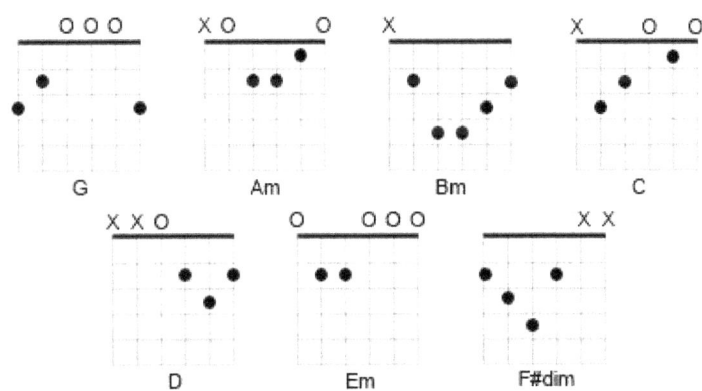

These different chords are a set of harmonically based combinations of notes that give a different "mood" For example the MAJOR chords are lively while the minor ones are moody. There are a vast number of these chords that provide these frequency variations of mood. For example for the

A MAJOR chord variations can include the minor Am, diminished Adim, A seventh or A7 as you will see in the table in the back of the song book and also further on in this lesson. Most of the time these add to the mood and song detail beyond the MAJOR chords.

You have become familiar with the Key of G and the MAJOR chords G D C. Now let us learn a few of these odd chords to see how they change the mood of the song. So three easy ones are Em A7 and D7. Like before, learn to play these easily and clear.

Learn to be comfortable with these three new chords, then try playing the song and singing it. You will see how the E minor and 7th chords change the sound. All the different variations of the major chords are shown on the inside of the book cover. Note the configuration of A7 where the first finger 1 is used on three strings. It mean hold the end part of the 1st finger against all three (also the bottom one if you wish because the 2nd finger covers the next fret)

So on this song, after you have learned these new chords try pickin and strumin' song 15 in the book.

Don't Think Twice

G   D   Em
It ain't no use to sit and wonder why babe
C   D7
It don't matter any how
G   D   Em
Ain't no use to sit and wonder why babe
C   D7
If you don't know by now
                  G   G7
When the rooster crows at the break of dawn
C   A7
Look out your window and I'll be gone
G   Em   C
You're the reason I'm travellin on
G   D7   G
Don't think twice, it's all right

You can play this as a great 1 2 Sokkie beat fast or slow. You can also simply play the G D C chords only, then play it again with the new chords to see how these other the chords changes the "mood".

Now you are ready to go to any favorite song and start your pickin' strummin' and grinnin'

Have Fun!

Oh, one more thing, always keep your guitar tuned!

One of the handiest devices is the Fender Clip On Guitar Tuner

It is well worth the $20 to have this device that simply clips onto your guitar and you can tune the strings perfectly in minutes.

Here are some more handy dandy charts and ideas to make your playing fun and easy.

HANDY CHORD CONVERSION CHART

This was our 7 chords for each Key:

KEY	M1	M1	M2	M2	M3	M3	D1
C	C	Dm	Em	F	G	Am	Bd
D	D	Em	Fm	G	A	Bm	C#d
E	E	F#m	G#m	A	B	C#m	D#d
F	F	Gm	Am	Bb	C	Dm	Ed
G	G	Am	Bm	C	D	Em	F#d
A	A	Bm	C#m	D	E	F#m	G#d
B	B	C#m	D#m	E	F#	G#m	A#m

If we rearrange the table, it becomes easy to convert the chords of one key to the other. For example suppose we had a song that was done in the key D and wanted to convert it to our key of G.

KEY	A	D	G	C	F	E
Major	A	D	**G**	C	F	E
minor	Bm	Em	**Am**	Dm	Gm	F#m
minor	C#m	Fm	**Bm**	Em	Am	G#m
Major	D	G	**C**	F	Bb	A
Major	E	A	**D**	G	C	B
minor	F#m	Bm	**Em**	Am	Dm	C#m
dim	G#d	C#d	**F#d**	Bd	Ed	D#d

Whenever you had a D, you would substitute G, Em would become Am, Fm would become Bm, G would become C, A would become D, Bm would become

Em and C#dim would become F#d. If you encountered a D7, it would be G7. And A7 would become D7.

HANDY DANDY CHORD CHART

GUITAR CHORD CHART

	MAJOR	MINOR	MAJ. 6th	MIN. 6th	DOM. 7th	MAJ. 7th	AUG. 7th	MIN 7th	AUG. (+)	DIM. (o)
C	C	Cm	C6	Cm6	C7	Cmaj7	C7+5	Cm7	C+	Cdim
Db or C#	Db	Dbm	Db6	Dbm6	Db7	Dbmaj7	Db7+5	Dbm7	Db+	Dbdim
D	D	Dm	D6	Dm6	D7	Dmaj7	D7+5	Dm7	D+	Ddim
Eb	Eb	Ebm	Eb6	Ebm6	Eb7	Ebmaj7	Eb7+5	Ebm7	Eb+	Ebdim
E	E	Em	E6	Em6	E7	Emaj7	E7+5	Em7	E+	Edim
F	F	Fm	F6	Fm6	F7	Fmaj7	F7+5	Fm7	F+	Fdim
Gb or F#	Gb	Gbm	Gb6	Gbm6	Gb7	Gbmaj7	Gb7+5	Gbm7	Gb+	Gbdim
G	G	Gm	G6	Gm6	G7	Gmaj7	G7+5	Gm7	G+	Gdim
Ab	Ab	Abm	Ab6	Abm6	Ab7	Abmaj7	Ab7+5	Abm7	Ab+	Abdim
A	A	Am	A6	Am6	A7	Amaj7	A7+5	Am7	A+	Adim
Bb	Bb	Bbm	Bb6	Bbm6	Bb7	Bbmaj7	Bb7+5	Bbm7	Bb+	Bbdim
B	B	Bm	B6	Bm6	B7	Bmaj7	B7+5	Bm7	B+	Bdim

Now, as a final note, I want to talk about the Key of C which has G, C, F as its MAJOR chords. This would add the F chord to your inventory and it is well worth learning this chord well.

Once again, the usual way this chord is taught is to cover the 1st and 2nd strings with the first finger (like you did in the A7 and leave the top 6th string open. Do not get used to this and follow the convention below for F. either you have a big finger and can cover all the strings with the first finger, or you can use your Thumb to cover the 6th string like you did for D

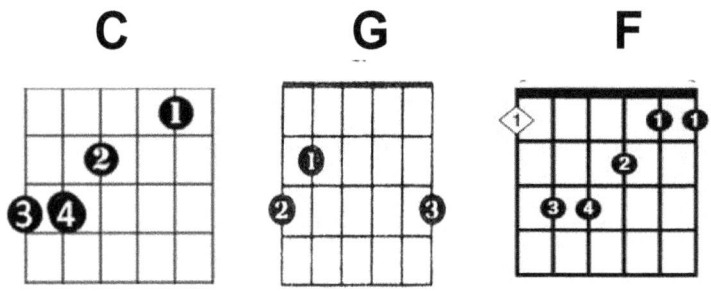

There are a few interesting things about this chord. First because it covers all strings, it can be positioned anywhere on the neck of the guitar. In the first fret position, it is F Major, in the second fret position it become F# Major. In the 3rd fret position it becomes G Major, in the 4th fret position it is G# or Ab, and in the 5th fret position it becomes A Major, and so on. This is the same effect a using a clamp called a Capo to shorten the strings and change the chord sound to a different one.

So if you played G your old way, and then moved your F chord configuration to the 3rd fret, they would sound the same. Try it

The other interesting thing about the Key of C is that for Runs and picking melodies all of the main notes are within easy movement of the first three frets and the picking and strumming is much easier.

HANDY DANDY TUNING YOUR GUITAR

How to Tune a Guitar

Tuning the guitar is vital to sounding good. Here are some simple instructions that explain guitar tuning basics. The open strings of a guitar from the thickest to thinnest are as follows:

- **E – the thickest or lowest sounding string is known as the 6th string**
- **A – is the 5th**
- **D – is the 4th**
- **G – is the 3rd**
- **B – is the 2nd**
- **E – the thinnest or highest is the 1st**

The most common method for tuning both Electric and Acoustic guitars – and the one you can use when no other instrument or guitar tuner is at hand is:

Standard Guitar Tuning Method

Step 1: The E String
Tune the thick **E**, as accurately as you can. If you have another instrument such as a Piano (which stays in tune for years), you can tune it to the 2nd **E** below middle **C.** If you have no device or instrument handy just try to get it as accurate as possible, what really counts when you are playing

is that the guitar is in tune with itself and any other instruments you might be playing with.

Step 2: The A String

Place the first finger of your left hand just behind the fifth fret on the bottom **E** string. That's an **A** note. Keep your finger on that fret. Now pick the fifth and six strings in turn, gently adjusting the fifth string tuning peg until the two notes are the same.

Step 3: The D String

Place the first finger of your left hand just behind the fifth fret on the **A** string. That's a **D** note. Tune the 4th string (the **D** note) to that.

Step 4: The G String

Place the first finger of your left hand just behind the fifth fret on the **D** string. That's a **G** note. Tune your **G** string to that note.

Step 5: The B String
Place the first finger of your left hand just behind the forth fret (note the **B** string is the only one that comes from a different position the forth fret, the rest are from the 5th fret).

Step 6: Tuning the E String
Place the first finger of your left hand just behind the fifth fret on the **B** string. That's an **E** note.

The other way is to use your phone or get onto YouTube and just follow the instructions. Here is a good example.

https://www.youtube.com/watch?v=jJxRjWtwmEE

Better still, treat yourself to a Fender Tuner!

Here's to strummin' and grinnin'

Have fun

Ed

www.ingramcontent.com/pod-product-compliance
Lightning Source LLC
Chambersburg PA
CBHW051711090426
42736CB00013B/2648